Fiction 4

Series Editor: Pie Corbett

CAMBRIDGE
UNIVERSITY PRESS

CAMBRIDGE UNIVERSITY PRESS
Cambridge, New York, Melbourne, Madrid, Cape Town, Singapore, São Paulo

Cambridge University Press
The Edinburgh Building, Cambridge CB2 2RU, UK

www.cambridge.org
Information on this title: www.cambridge.org/9780521618861

First published 2006

Printed in the United Kingdom at the University Press, Cambridge

A catalogue record for this publication is available from the British Library

ISBN-13 978-0-521-61886-1 paperback
ISBN-10 0-521-61886-X paperback

ACKNOWLEDGEMENTS

Cover

Beehive Illustration (Pulsar Studio)

Artwork

Beehive Illustration (Pulsar Studio)

Texts

Historical stories: 'A Bit of Blue Sky' by Chris Buckton

Sci-fi/Fantasy: 'The Seekers' by Valerie Bloom

Stories from other cultures: 'Old Man Shoa and the Fire' by Thomas Munro

Contents

Historical stories

A Bit of Blue Sky

Chapter One

Meet the Family

Benjamin, age 8

I'm Benjie. My father died last year and my mother couldn't afford to keep us all. So she took three of us down to the workhouse. My sister howled because they took her to the bathroom first and scrubbed her something cruel. My brother and I went in a bath together, and then they put clean clothes on us. Rough, they were, brown and scratchy. I did cry a bit too when our mam left us. I did wonder if I'd ever see her again.

Eliza, age 9

I'm Lizzie. I begged and pleaded with our mam not to take us to the workhouse but what could she do? She had no money and six of us to feed. She said it was for the best, that we'd be fed and we'd be taught a trade. I know she loves us, but she had to keep the babies and let us go.

I couldn't stop from blubbing when they cropped my hair as if I was a sheep. At tea time I thought of our little cottage and the fire going and mam feeding the baby. In here we all sit on long benches and we can't talk. We had bread and cheese tonight but I couldn't eat for crying.

Thomas, age 11

I'm Thomas. I'm the eldest of our family and I try to look after Benjie and Lizzie. Specially Lizzie, for she's lame. When my dad was dying he said that I was the man now. But it's hard being taken away from home and treated like a child. I have a quick temper on me that leads me astray over and over.

We walked up to the workhouse. There's a great wall all around it, and I had to pull the bell rope at the gates. The porter looked at us like we were vermin. When we came in, they took all our things – not that we had much. Just Benjie's penny whistle, Lizzie's sewing and my whittling knife.

We had to go before the Guardians, standing in a row with our knees knocking. Some fat starchy ladies and gentlemen looked us up and down and told us we should be grateful to the

Parish. Then they wrote in a book but we didn't know how to sign our names. We just put a cross. I wonder what they thought of us.

One good thing, they give us boots. We only had one pair between us when we come, and those had the soles flapping loose from all of us children wearing them out. Mostly we had to go barefoot. Bad in winter, and my chilblains itched at night. So new boots were good. They say they'll school us, too. I would like that. I've never been to school, we didn't have the boots and we didn't have the money.

Chapter Two

Settling In

Benjie

In the morning they ring a bell and we have to stand by our beds. My belly is so empty, it feels like paper stuck together. Porridge for breakfast, thin and grey and tasting of dishwater. Porridge and a piece of dry bread.

Then to the school room. We sat on long benches and I couldn't see out of the windows, they were too high. My heart beat hard when the master called me out to the front. I couldn't write my name on the board and I could hear the other boys laughing. But I'm going to learn.

The master is kind and smiles and lays his hand on my head and says "Strive, strive, my boy." He was in the workhouse when he was a lad and he bettered himself. He went off to London town and trained for a teacher. And now he's back with a suit of good cloth and shiny boots. I'm going to better myself, I am.

Lizzie

The workhouse is like some great grey church. The tall clocktower seems to be frowning at me. The building is full of dark corners and the smell of washing. The stone stairs up to bed are all worn in the middle. It makes me sad to think of all those lonely children's feet going up them. And it's strange not being in our big brass bed with my sisters to keep me warm. There's rows of us here, but all separate, in little iron beds.

What I can't bear is that I can't be with Thomas and Benjie. The boys go one way and the girls the other. We don't see each other except at meal times and on Sundays. This morning I could see little Benjie at breakfast and he was crying, "I want Lizzie." It fair broke my heart. But he's got Thomas there with him, which is something. And there's a big girl who has the bed next to mine, Mags she's called, and she has a bad leg like me. She has a brother too, maybe he'll look out for my two.

Mags says it's not so bad here if you keep on the straight and narrow. She says we'll get taught how to sew and then we'll get a wage when we're old enough.

Thomas

It's true, they do school us. The schoolroom's warm with a big stove in the middle. There's a text on the wall saying The World is Full of Beautiful Things. Not in here, it's not.

I sat with a boy called Matthew who doesn't care what he says or does. He whispered to me how he absconded, that's run away I think. But they caught him and put him in the punishment cell. In the afternoon we went to the workshop to learn to make shoes. Hard work it was, and I got rapped on the knuckles for looking out the window but I picked it up fast.

Chapter Three

Light and Dark

Benjie

This day was a mix of good and very bad. The good was strange, I'll tell you what it was.

We were in the schoolroom doing our reading. I like that, and I can write my name now. Teacher says if I work hard I'll get a trade, and not be at the mercy of the farmer, like my poor dad was. The farmer was a cruel man, he worked my dad so hard and gave him so little.

While we were sitting at our work, in came a lady dressed in black with a veil hiding her face. We all had to stand and say good morning to her. Some of us read out loud from the bible. She walked between our desks looking at our work, and when she came to my desk, she stopped. She put her hand under my chin to lift my face. "So like my Alexander," she whispered. Her voice was full of sadness. She asked my name, and lifted her veil, and kissed me. "Bless you Benjamin," she said, and then she was gone.

The master told us we had done well. "That lady is the vicar's wife," he said. "She lost her boy to the smallpox a few months past." She stayed in my mind. Nobody had kissed me since we were with our mother.

But you remember I said this day was good and very bad, and I haven't told you the very bad yet. They put my brother Thomas in the punishment cell. And they thrashed me for shouting out against it.

Lizzie

Thomas did something for my sake today, but he's paid dearly for it and so has Benjie. It's not fair. When we came out of supper, some children who didn't know any better were scoffing and laughing at my leg, and my hopping walk. And Thomas took them on,

even though they were great lads, and he bloodied their noses. The Master come up with a scowl and said Thomas was disorderly. Next thing I know, Thomas has knocked the Master's cap off.

Thomas

It's dark in here, and cold, and there's a scrabbly noise which must be rats. Though what rats would hope to find here I don't know, seeing as how I've eaten every crumb of the bread they gave me. I'm in this cell for 48 hours, with nothing but bread and water. They say I'm refractory.

It's too harsh, and it's wrong, but they won't break my spirit. My body may be cold but my heart is red hot with anger.

Chapter Four

What Can We Do?

Benjie

There's nothing for it but to get out of this place. I can't stand to see Thomas brought so low. The master stood up in hall when Thomas was let out, and pointed at him. "This boy is a disgrace. He should hang his head in shame," he said, in front of everyone. "Keep away from him, he will lead you into mischief." But Thomas wouldn't hang his head. For that he got a thrashing.

The lads are on to Lizzie now that they know that Thomas can't touch them. Every day they go behind her, aping her limp. And they try to trip her. The kind master has left, and instead we have a man with a whip who teaches us nothing.

If I could get out, I could find the lady who kissed me. I could beg her to help us. I could climb over the wall. I'd have to wait till dark, and maybe Matthew could give me a leg up. And I'm not watched all the time, like Thomas is. It would be easy to slip away. And what's more, it's me that could melt the vicar's wife's heart.

Lizzie

What Thomas did has made us all bad, it seems. When we met after church on Sunday, we all agreed we couldn't bear it here any longer. I try my best with the sewing but now they make me scrub floors, which is cruel on my leg.

If it weren't for Mags I don't know what I'd do. She says it'll all turn out for the best. She and Matthew are hoping that their big sister will come for them. She's got a post as maid to the vicar's wife. She's getting married to the gardener and she'll have a cottage of her own. But I'm feeling that nobody knows or cares that we're here, not even our mother. I would write her a letter but she can't read…

But say I wrote to the vicar's wife? I could tell her how we want to be back home, and how my sewing is good enough now to take in work and earn something.

Thomas

I can't forget – they took away my pride in myself. But I'll show them. My friend Matthew got out. I know he got caught again, but maybe I'd have better luck. He says I could hide in the cart that comes over from the farm to bring our potatoes. If I hid under the sacks I could jump off when we were outside the gates.

Chapter Five

Escape!

Benjie

I've done it! I'm over the wall! Running like the blazes, stumbling in the dark. I can find my way to the vicarage because I know that it will be near the church, and I can see the spire up above the trees.

Here it is. Such a grand house, with a driveway up to the porch. There are lights in some of the windows. I take the heavy door knocker in both hands and crack it down as hard as I can.

It's a maid who opens the door. She gasps

when she sees me. "You're from the workhouse!" She knows it from my uniform. "Do you know my brother Matthew?" She looks frightened and tries to bundle me out. "You'll get me in trouble!" she whispers. But I hear a gentle voice. "Aggie, who is it?" And the lady in black comes to the door. "Bless my soul!" she says when she sees me. "Oh my lady, help us. It's not right what they do to us!" And I fall down by her feet.

Lizzie

Oh what a going-on there's been! The vicar's wife came up, and she brought the vicar. They had our Benjie with them. We were sent for, Thomas and me. She is taking us into her care. I cannot believe it's true. I will be maid of all work, but no scrubbing floors. Thomas will work in the garden, Benjie is to be errand boy. And we will see mother every week.

But I feel sad for those we leave behind. What help will they have?

Thomas

Well, I don't know as if I've done what my pa wanted me to do, but our family are back together again. Not thanks to me, although Lizzie says it was, in a way. Best of all, is to see the sky and the fields. The vicar says to hold my head up high. And I shall do.

THE SEEKERS

CHAPTER ONE

Long ago, the peaceful kingdom of Raban was conquered by the Digons, and the people were enslaved. To save the kingdom from eternal slavery, the Watcher had taken the sacred stones of Raban away from the Sanctuary to a secret hiding place. These precious stones had remained hidden for many long years, but the Raban scrolls, which described the history and the future of the kingdom, told how one day the Chosen One would find the stones and bring light and peace back to the kingdom. When he or she came, the Digons would be defeated and slavery would end. The Digons would do their utmost to stop the Chosen One – but would not succeed.

Each year, the Guardians selected a young person to go on a quest to find the sacred stones, and each year they hoped that this boy or girl might be the Chosen One. So far, all had returned from the journey empty-handed.

To be selected for the quest was a great honour for any boy or girl of Raban, but first they had to prove themselves in the trials.

Kehan was surprised at how well he had done in this year's trials. He had answered all the questions about the scrolls confidently. But then, he had almost memorised them in preparing for the day. It was the endurance test that he'd been dreading. Nevertheless, he had been able to lift a basketful of conchi nuts and carry it a hundred metres to the storehouse, stopping only once. Horaf, naturally, had carried two baskets without stopping, as if the giant nuts were no heavier than feathers.

Now they were waiting. Everyone knew that Horaf, the strongest and the biggest, would be the one going on the quest. But secretly, each youth was hoping to be picked.

"What's taking them so long?" said Horaf.

Kehan looked at him.

"They are only a little late," he said. "Be patient."

"It's easy for you to talk about patience," Horaf scoffed. "It's obvious you won't be chosen."

Bariel defended her friend.

"You speak as if you have already been picked. Anyone could be going on the journey – and anyone could be the Chosen One. Kehan has as much chance as you."

Horaf was dismissive.

"Hah!" he said, "The Chosen One must be courageous and strong. No one would think a weak scholar was meant to save our people."

Kehan looked away. Horaf was right. He was not just weaker than most others, he was the smallest of them all. He could never be picked for the journey, let alone be the Chosen One.

The door opened. The second Guardian stood in the doorway with the three seekers' rods in her hand. These had power to guide and protect any who went in search of the stones.

"Kehan of Daveed," she said," you are to go on this year's quest. Step forward."

Kehan could not believe his ears. He glanced at Horaf, who was standing like a statue, staring at the Guardian.

"Kehan, come forward."

The second Guardian spoke again, and Kehan felt Bariel nudge him in the ribs.

"Go!" his friend hissed.

The Guardian handed him the red and blue striped rod.

"You have done well," she said. "You are ready for the journey. Choose your companions."

The other youths were watching Kehan hopefully.

"I choose Bariel of Daveed," he said. How could he not choose his friend? He paused. He should choose someone else from the House of Daveed. It was expected. But what about Horaf? He'd been so disappointed not to be chosen. But he was of the House of Sauul. The two houses had never gone on the quest together. Kehan tangled his index finger through his long locks, as he did whenever he was thinking.

"And the other?" the second Guardian asked.

Kehan took a deep breath, then spoke clearly, and louder than he'd meant to.

"I choose Horaf."

There was an immediate hum of surprise around him as people took in what this meant. For the first time, the Houses of Daveed and Sauul would make the journey together.

Kehan caught a glimpse of Horaf, standing with his arms folded and his head angled slightly upward, in a pose that seemed to say, "Why are you all so surprised? I should be the leader on this journey, not just a companion."

The three were soon furnished with food, and each one given a rod. They would need to go quickly to make the most of the poor daylight. Since the sacred stones had gone, Raban's days were short and the two suns never shone with their full light. The first Guardian spoke.

"You must choose a route for yourselves, but first decide how you will travel. What is the decision, Kehan?"

Kehan paused and eyed the shimmering black horses before them. How much easier and faster the journey would be on horseback. And he knew that Horaf could outride anyone.

But Bariel was an inexperienced rider. He also knew from the scrolls that the journey might involve moments where they needed to be still and quiet, and to pass through narrow, dangerous spaces. The horses would be no help then. Would it be better to travel as they were, on foot?

CHOICE 1 Travel on horseback (Go to page 25.)

CHOICE 2 Travel on foot (Go to page 27.)

CHOICE 1

Travel on horseback

They galloped out of the village, excited and full of energy, then slowed to a trot.

"Horaf! Why him?" Bariel looked across at Kehan, out of breath and a little off-balance on the handsome horse. Kehan shrugged.

"He was disappointed that he wasn't picked. I thought this would make him feel better."

"We've never had a journey with people from the two Houses together. There's bound to be trouble."

Kehan sighed. He was afraid Bariel was right. Since they'd left the Sanctuary and the crowds of the village square, Horaf had darted ahead, his lips tight and eyes steely. After the first startled glance, he had not looked at Kehan. Now he was several metres ahead. This bothered Kehan. He should be leading, not Horaf. Bariel obviously thought so as well.

"Anyone would think he had been chosen for the quest," she muttered, wiping the sweat from her forehead.

Horaf had come to the familiar fork at the end of the long, winding road from their village. He seemed about to ride along one of the paths, but Kehan quickened to catch up with him.

"Horaf, wait. I have not yet decided which way to go."

Horaf stopped and turned to face them.

"Why do you keep pretending? You were not trained for this. You know the choosing was a mistake. I have been trained and I do not need you to tell me where to go."

Kehan paused, on the edge of replying. As he looked to the left he could see a valley path winding through marshlands and dense forest; to the right, a narrow, rocky mountain track. Either way would be impossible for the horses. They would have to be left behind. Kehan could feel the heat rising through his face, but said nothing.

CHOICE 2

Travel on foot

"Are you sure you made the right choice?" Bariel nodded towards Horaf, who was several metres ahead, slashing at the gurano bushes with his blue rod as though battling an imaginary enemy. Kehan couldn't help wondering, though, if he was that enemy, and whether Horaf was still bitter about being a companion rather than the Chosen One. He sighed.

"We'll soon find out," he said.

"I don't need to wait. I can tell you now, he's not going to make this easy. He was convinced that we should have taken the horses."

"Well, Horaf won't want to come back a failure. We all want to find the stones, so we'll all have to work together."

Bariel gave a little smile.

"Yes, you're right. But just make sure Horaf doesn't go off on his own little journey. Who knows? He might find the stones without you."

Horaf came to a stop and turned towards them.

"If we want to get anywhere before nightfall, I suggest we keep up speed," he said, bitterly.

"You're right, Horaf. But remember, we need strength for the trials ahead."

"And I don't think the Guardians meant us to use our rods to fight harmless gurano bushes," Bariel added.

Horaf clutched his rod tighter and walked on stiffly, then stopped at a fork in the road. The three of them stood for a few moments, judging each route. To the left they could see a valley path winding through marshlands and dense forest; to the right, a narrow, rocky mountain track. Which way should they go?

CHAPTER TWO

To their right, a narrow, rocky track wound, snake-like, up the side of the mountain. That great gloomy rock had been a familiar sight from the village and from the towers of the Sanctuary. To their left, the boggy path curved lazily round the side of the dense, murky Forest of Gheza towards the valley. They would have to take one of the two.

Kehan wondered whether they could handle the rocky mountain route. Then again, parts of the valley might be flooded at this time of year. He looked around at his companions.

"I'm not really sure," said Bariel, looking unimpressed by both routes.

Horaf was already facing one path, as though his mind was made up. Kehan thought about asking his advice, but Horaf didn't seem to be in the mood for talk.

Which way? Kehan wondered. The choice was his alone.

CHOICE 1 Take the mountain path (Go to page 30.)

CHOICE 2 Take the valley path (Go to page 33.)

CHOICE 1

Take the mountain path

The path was narrow. It rose steeply and the sharp rocks were painful against their bare feet, but Kehan hardly noticed. He was trying to remember all he had read of the Chosen One's journey.

Halfway up the mountain he stopped.

"Can you hear that?" he asked. Bariel and Horaf stopped and listened.

"You're imagining things," Horaf said. "I can't hear anything."

"Neither can I," Bariel said.

"I think the hounds are coming," Kehan continued.

"The hounds live in the valley," Horaf laughed scornfully. "If you had listened to the Guardian's directions instead of having your head in a scroll all the time, you would have known that."

"We're ready for them, whatever they are!" Bariel cried.

Kehan peered down at where the path fell off into a steep precipice. All he could see were the silver tops of the warnor trees. Far below, all was darkness. Nothing stirred. He shrugged and turned back towards the path.

"Perhaps you are right," he said.

Suddenly there was a chorus of howls and yelps from the foot of the mountain. "The hounds!" Kehan looked desperately around for a place from which to fight.

"I told you this was the wrong path," Horaf scowled at Kehan. "We cannot fight here."

"Stand close together and use your rods," Kehan said.

The sound of the beasts was enough to strike fear into the heart of the bravest warrior. But the sight was worse. They stood six feet tall on legs like thick branches. Their mouths were huge caverns; their teeth were like spears, and their eyes looked as if fires were lit in them. They stood silently watching the three companions. Kehan was having difficulty breathing. He felt Bariel tremble beside him. Horaf stiffened, sweat trickling slowly down his forehead. Then the hounds charged.

The three companions hit out with their rods. Bariel hit one hound across its snout. Kehan caught another round its ear. The hounds yelped and withdrew for a second. Howling, they charged again. At that moment, Kehan heard something. A strange voice seemed to be whispering to him.

"Stand behind me!" he yelled. "Give me your rods!"

"Are you mad?" Horaf did not take his eyes from the hound galloping towards him. Bariel stared at Kehan, then silently handed him her rod.

"You too!" she screamed at Horaf.

Kehan held the rods together and waited. The hounds streaked towards him. His palms were wet, and his hands shaking. When he could see his reflection in their eyes, he clashed the rods together. Blinding light lit up the mountainside. Yelping in agony, the hounds reeled backward and tumbled over the side into the darkness below.

CHOICE 2

Take the valley path

Horaf hurried on towards the
valley, as though challenging
them to keep up with him. He
had wanted to take the other
path, and now he seemed less
and less happy to be part of the
group. Then suddenly he came
to a stop.

"What is it?" Kehan called.

"Look!" Horaf pointed to the
chasm before them. It was about
fifty metres wide and seemed
bottomless, stretching as far as
they could see in both directions.

Suddenly the air was split by a spine-chilling sound, part
howl and part shriek. "I knew they would find us in the valley,"
Horaf said quietly. Kehan looked around frantically. There was
nowhere to hide.

"Here they come!" Bariel shouted.

The three companions crouched, their rods ready. Three shapes appeared in front of them. They had the heads of hounds, but their huge open jaws revealed forked tongues that flicked the air as they approached. Their cat-like bodies were covered in green scales, the large feet ending in massive claws. Their eyes burned.

"What are they?" whispered Bariel.

Kehan swallowed. He had read about them in the scrolls.

"Misstraals," he said.

"Well, I … I think we should attack now," Bariel stammered. "They're no match for us."

"This isn't the time for empty words, Bariel. We need to be calm and wait for the right moment." Horaf spoke quietly, his eyes never leaving the creatures.

The creatures were crouched. Kehan's palms were sweaty and his rod slipped, knocking into Bariel's. A spark flew from the place where they touched. He remembered the scrolls.

"Put the rods together!" he shouted, as the animals leapt.

They were knocked off their feet and fell dangerously close to the edge of the ravine, but as they fell, Bariel's rod clashed with Kehan's. There was a flash of light and the mistraals retreated with frustrated howls. The three youths scrambled to their feet.

"The rods!" Kehan yelled. "Bring them together."

The rods blazed as they made contact. Snarling, the mistraals backed away.

"We must lead them to the ravine," Kehan continued. "Walk slowly towards them. Then, when I give the signal, turn and run. Stop at the edge of the ravine, dig your rods into the ground and jump." He looked into the faces of his companions. Horaf's expression seemed to be saying, "Why should we listen to you?"

"Trust me," Kehan said.

They took three paces towards the retreating beasts. When they felt the hot breath of the mistraals on their faces, Kehan yelled, "Run!"

They sprinted towards the ravine, swifter than arrows. Then, as they came to its edge, Kehan gave the command, "Jump!"

The rods lifted them high into the air. Bariel gasped.

"We're flying!"

They landed softly on the other side. Behind them the howls stopped. They turned to see the last swishing tail disappearing into the ravine.

CHAPTER THREE

They slumped, shaking, onto the path. No one spoke. After a while, Kehan rose. The two suns were halfway across the sky on their journey north.

"Let's go," Kehan said. Bariel stood beside him.

"We weren't told about those animals," she said quietly.

"It's in the scrolls," Kehan replied.

"And the touching rods?" Horaf asked suddenly.

Kehan frowned.

"No, I was told to do that as we were fighting."

Horaf stared.

"Who told you?"

Kehan thought for a moment.

"I don't know," he said.

They came to the valley of Mizra.

"The Watcher's house is up there," Kehan said. Was this the moment when they would find

the stones? The scrolls described how the Chosen One should call the Watcher and seek his advice.

"Should we call him now?" Bariel asked.

"Not yet. Wait until we reach the house. Remember, the Watcher cannot look at the suns. He must hide his eyes until the stones have been returned to Raban."

Horaf was eyeing the tall building.

"This doesn't look like a place for the Watcher of Raban," he said. "Look at how those windows are left wide open to the light."

Kehan said nothing. He wasn't eager to go near the building, but he knew that they had to light a fire by the door to call the Watcher. Soon, they had gathered branches and a small fire crackled before them. The dancing flames were reflected on the lake behind the house, but they couldn't penetrate the gloom. The door creaked open. A shadow stood there, covered from head to toe in a dark hooded robe, its face hidden. Kehan moved reluctantly towards the shape.

"Who calls the Watcher?" Its voice was hoarse.

"The seekers of Raban," Kehan answered. "We seek the stones."

The figure laughed, a dry rasping sound like a cough.

"Many seek the stones," it said.

"But only one will find them," Kehan responded.

"That's the way." The figure pointed a bony finger the way they had just come. Kehan looked at the pale hand.

"You're not the Watcher," he said. The figure threw back his hood and straightened.

"So, a clever seeker of Raban!"

The companions stepped back as the mysterious figure was revealed. His face was pale as alabaster; his eyes were flames. He towered above them. Kehan knew they had two choices. They could find the strength to walk away, or they could fight.

CHOICE 1 Walk away (Go to page 39.)
CHOICE 2 Fight (Go to page 41.)

CHOICE 1

Walk away

"Who are you?"

"Where is the Watcher?"

Bariel and Horaf spoke together. The figure laughed, a loud booming laugh like a thunderclap. "The Watcher sleeps. As for who I am," he turned to Kehan, "why don't you ask your companion. You know, don't you, young seeker?"

"He's the Negatron." Kehan clutched his rod tighter. "We don't seek to fight you. Our business is with the Watcher."

"Hmmm." The Negatron looked thoughtful and twisted his silver locks around his finger in the same way Kehan did when he was thinking. Kehan felt his eyes getting heavy and a numbness stealing over his mind. At that moment, he heard a hissing whisper: "You don't want the stones."

"I don't want the stones," Kehan said, drowsily.

"You are just a scholar. You are not trained for this." The Negatron continued his hypnotic words. He was looking at Horaf, but speaking to Kehan. Horaf looked away guiltily.

"I am just a…"

"No!" Horaf grabbed hold of Kehan and shook him. He knew how the Negatron played with people's minds.

"You are Kehan of Daveed, and you have been chosen for the quest."

Slowly the fog lifted from Kehan's mind.

"I am Kehan of Daveed." He stared at the Negatron. The Negatron scowled. Bariel looked on, slowly beginning to understand what had happened. Horaf had helped Kehan at a crucial time. The question was, would Kehan be strong enough to lead them onwards?

CHOICE 2

Fight

"What is it?" Bariel whispered.

"He's the Negatron," said Kehan.

"Careful what you think," added Horaf. "He'll use your thoughts against you."

At that moment the figure turned to Horaf, his lips moving. Horaf doubled up, clutching his stomach in agony.

"Leave him alone!" Kehan darted at the Negatron. His rod connected with its head and Horaf fell to the ground. The Negatron turned towards Kehan, who lashed out with his rod again. He looked anxiously towards Horaf, who was getting groggily to his feet.

"Kehan, watch out!" Bariel shouted. The Negatron was right next to him and its bony fingers were reaching towards his forehead. Kehan reached up and grabbed hold of the hand. It was ice-cold and slippery. He struggled to hold on to it, for he knew that the moment the Negatron touched his head, it would control him.

"Thwack!" Bariel's rod came down at the same time as Horaf's. They clashed into each other and sparks flew. The Negatron reeled and staggered away from Kehan.

"Rods together!" Kehan yelled.

The rods glowed. The Negatron retreated then turned back towards them. The three companions held their rods upright like a shield.

Bariel looked across at Kehan and Horaf. They had all helped each other. Did this mean they were now a team? And was Kehan safe from the Negatron?

CHAPTER FOUR

"We'll find the stones ourselves," Kehan said. He felt the Negatron trying to enter his mind. Icy fingers, probing his brain. "You cannot come in," he thought. He heard the voice in his head like the hissing of a snake:

"You do not want the stones. You want to s-s-s-sleep, s-s-s-sleep, s-s-s-sleep..."

It took all his will to resist.

"I am Kehan. You cannot come in. I have been chosen for the quest." He repeated the words in his head. At last the Negatron gave a whimper of defeat and Kehan felt the fingers loosen and fall away. He closed his eyes with relief but they flew open again at the gasps from his two companions.

The Negatron was shrinking. The robe crumpled around its feet. In seconds it was like a small child. With a shriek it turned and scampered back into the building. They watched in quiet amazement. At last Bariel spoke.

"Should we go and see if the Watcher lives?"

The others could tell she didn't want to.

"He'll be fine," Kehan said. "The Negatron's weak, but we must hurry before he gets his strength back. The suns are setting. We don't want to be outside the Sanctuary after dark."

"Where do we go?" Horaf asked.

"We must cross the lake. Perhaps there is a bridge."

There was no bridge. Moored to a warnor tree there was a small boat, but it was old. It might not be safe. The only alternative was a tunnel that went under the lake. That way would be quick but it would be dark, and fierce Digon creatures could be sleeping there.

CHOICE 1 Use the boat (Go to page 45.)

CHOICE 2 Use the tunnel (Go to page 47.)

CHOICE 1

Use the boat

They were in the middle of the lake. Horaf and Bariel were rowing with the oars they had found in the bottom of the boat. Kehan crouched in the bow, shouting directions. He was thinking they might make it across the lake without mishap when Horaf gave a yell. Kehan spun round.

"Look!" Horaf was pointing to the bottom of the boat. A slim but deadly sharp silver saw was cutting a hole in the wood, and the green water was oozing through.

"We have to stop it!" Bariel shouted, "Or we'll drown."

Horaf tried to beat off the mysterious attacker with his oar, but whatever it was did not even pause.

"Oh, no!"

Bariel was pointing at the sides of the boat. There were several silver saws busily cutting holes all around them, and now the vessel was beginning to sink. Kehan glanced over the side and saw two beady eyes looking back at him with a piercing stare. The water was swarming with cutterfish. If they didn't drown the cutterfish would soon finish them, either with the saws on their snouts or with the lethal razors they had for fins.

As he looked around desperately, Kehan's eyes fell on the rods at the bottom of the boat. Something clicked in his mind. He grabbed them and plunged them together into the lake. The waters hissed and foamed. The cutterfish screamed and vanished. A giant wave lifted the boat high into the air.

"The rods!" Bariel screamed. "Take them out!"

"I'm trying!" Kehan was panting with the effort. "They're too heavy."

Horaf rose to help, but at that moment the wave sped towards the shore and threw them on the sand. Kehan felt the rods wrenched from his hands. The wave receded, taking the rods with it.

They scrambled up, drenched and spluttering. The boat was in splinters, but for a while all they could think about was catching their breath. They were simply grateful to be on solid ground. Then Kehan remembered what had happened – and began to worry.

CHOICE 2

Use the tunnel

The tunnel was dark. They could hardly see their hands in front of their faces. "We'd better use the rods," Kehan said.

They walked in single file, Kehan at the front with the rods lighting the way. The sandy floor was littered with bones and broken shells which dug painfully into their feet. Several corridors led away from the main passage through which they were travelling.

"I think I see a light," Kehan said after a while. "We must be nearing the other end." But then he saw that the light was actually a fire in the distance – and it was speeding towards them.

"Oh no!" Kehan groaned.

"What is it?" Bariel asked.

"It looks like a Digon firehorse," Horaf replied. "The rods will be useless against it, I think. It lives on fire."

"What do we do?" Bariel asked.

"Here!" Kehan handed out the rods. "Hit it as hard as you can."

The firehorse filled the tunnel. It was a gigantic, dark shape, with a flame at its centre. Horaf was right. The rods had no effect on it. Kehan felt its weight smothering him. He was burning up. The choking gasps coming from his friends told him they fared no better.

"Give me your rods," he cried, through parched lips. He groped for the rods and touched them to his. Then, with all his strength he rammed them against the firehorse.

There was a hissing sound. The animal pulled back, howling. Kehan and the others clamped their hands to their ears, their heads almost exploding from the noise.

"Look! It's melting!" said Bariel. A pool of water was gathering at their feet and rising rapidly.

"Run!" Horaf shouted. But before any of them could move, they were swept off their feet and carried through the passage by a great blast of air and water.

They were thrown, soaking and spluttering, on the shore. Shivering, they scrambled to their feet. It was then that Kehan realised what had happened – and began to worry.

CHAPTER FIVE

"I've lost the rods," Kehan whispered, his voice shaking.

Then out of nowhere, a voice answered, "The rods have done their work and are not needed any more." Kehan recognised the voice. It was the one that had given him directions on the journey.

They whirled round. Behind them was a man in a long blue robe. His hair was like a white halo around his head, and though he seemed to be watching them, his eyes were closed. He stood tall and leaned on a staff of red and blue stripes.

"Come, young seeker. You and your companions have done more than any other young seekers of Raban.

To complete your task, however, there is one more trial you must face."

Kehan stepped forward nervously, not sure whether he should speak. His throat felt tight, as though a hand was clamped around his neck. The old man began again.

"Tell me this. Where are the sacred stones? Do I hold them in my left hand or my right?"

Left or right? How could Kehan tell? Which should he choose?

CHOICE 1 Left hand (Go to page 51.)
CHOICE 2 Right hand (Go to page 52.)

CHOICE 1

Left hand

After touching the man's left hand, Kehan felt Bariel at his shoulder, breathing quickly, as though she had climbed a hill. Horaf, though, seemed to be holding his breath. The eyes of both were like arrows aimed at the old man's hands.

"I can't help thinking it's the right hand," Horaf whispered.

"Maybe the question is a trick," Bariel said. "He isn't another Negatron, is he?"

After what seemed like hours, the man smiled slowly. His left hand moved towards them, as if in slow motion. The long, slim fingers parted, and for a second they caught sight of a white light in the palm of his hand. Kehan thought he saw three round shapes in that light, but in a moment they were gone. And the old man's palm was empty.

What did it mean? Kehan's head was spinning. Had he failed this last trial? His heart pounded at the thought of failing now – after they had been through so much.

Go to page 53.

CHOICE 2

Right hand

"I never read about a test like this in the scrolls,' whispered Horaf.

"Maybe Kehan should have chosen the left hand instead," said Bariel. "It looks as  though there's something shining between his fingers."

Before Kehan could add his own thoughts, the old man broke into a smile. His left hand moved towards them, as if in slow motion. The long, slim fingers parted and they saw… nothing! It was empty. Was it too soon to celebrate? As the old man's right hand moved towards them, their eyes followed as though hypnotised. For a second they caught sight of a white light in the palm of his hand. Kehan thought he saw three round shapes in that light, but in a moment they were gone. And the old man's palm was empty.

What did it mean? Kehan's head was spinning. Had he failed this last trial? His heart pounded at the thought of failing now – after they had been through so much.

Go to page 53.

Chapter Five *continued*

The next moment, the old man pointed behind Kehan with his long bronze fingers.

"Take the stones. They are yours."

Kehan turned and stared. Barely half a metre from him was an altar. On it, three pearl-white stones, the size of gulls' eggs, glistened in the dusk.

"What is it?" Bariel asked.

"The stones." Kehan's voice was full of awe.

"Where?" Horaf seemed confused.

Kehan frowned.

"There. Can't you see them?"

Bariel and Horaf shook their heads. Kehan reached out and lifted the stones from the altar. As he touched them, a light spread over the shore, piercing the gathering darkness.

The man bowed to Kehan.

"The Watcher salutes the Chosen One," he said. "Peace can now return to Raban."

Kehan stood still in shock. "We've done it," he said to himself. "I was the Chosen One." Slowly, he turned smiling to his friends, the sacred stones shining in his hands.

Stories from other cultures

Old Man Shoa and The Fire

Chapter One

A long time ago, far off and high in the mountains, there lived an old man. He was a medicine man, a magic man, a shaman, and his name was Shoa.

Shoa lived in the misty forests of the Hmong country, with no house and no farm, and he had long wild hair and he ate wild fruit and drank the wild water from the running river. And he wore no clothes, and he had five friends. Their names were White Bear, Red Dragon, Brown Pig, Orange Tiger and Black Thunder. And they were all as wild as he was.

In those days, White Bear was all white, and Orange Tiger was a golden colour, without any stripes. Brown Pig was brown all over and his hair was not yellow as it is today.

Shoa's five friends hunted together, they slept on the forest floor together, and they laughed and played together, and boasted how smart they were. They were happy. But Old Man Shoa looked on as they played and hunted and laughed, and a dark light would come into his eyes. Then he would shake his head, as if he was trying to wake up from a dream. Sometimes at night, he sat up on a big rock looking at the bright stars over the forest. And while the dragon and the pig and tiger and the thunder and the bear slept, Old Man Shoa sighed and examined his shadow in the moonlight.

But he never told the others what was troubling him. He never boasted, either.

One day Red Dragon came to the others in the forest. He looked sad, even though the sun was shining through the trees.

"Friends," he told them. "I think I must leave you. I feel the Anger of Dragons growing up inside me, and I am afraid. I fear that my anger will grow too hot. I will shout and scream and fly like a mad thing through the forest, breaking down the trees and killing the animals. I must go away."

But his friends laughed at him.

"We are not afraid of you," said Old Man Shoa. "There is nothing you can do that can frighten us."

So saying, he snapped a twig in his fingers, and he used it to clean his fingernails.

"Watch then," said the dragon. And he flew up to the mountain top, and while the others watched, he screamed and shouted and ran mad and broke trees and split rocks. The whole Earth shook.

Then he came down again.

"That wasn't so bad," said Orange Tiger. "Stay with us. We are all as wild as you."

So the dragon stayed.

Chapter Two

The next day, when they were swimming in the river and the sun was making patterns of white and gold in the bamboo thicket, White Bear came down to the river bank. He looked at his friends and he smiled sadly.

"Friends," he said to them, "I know we told Red Dragon to stay with us. But I fear I must truly leave you. I feel the Rage of Bears inside me, and I am afraid it will burst out.

I will bellow and call and run mad through the forest, breaking down the trees and killing the animals. I must go away."

But his friends laughed up at him out of the brown water.

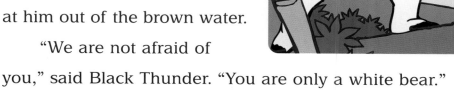

"We are not afraid of you," said Black Thunder. "You are only a white bear."

So the bear left them, and he went storming up through the shadows of the rhododendron trees, scattering parrots into the blue sky above. He crossed falling streams and scowled at the monkeys playing on the steaming stones. At last he came out on the top of the mountain, where the snakes lay among shimmering black rocks.

And then he bellowed and he called, and he tore up bushes and frightened the snakes into their dark holes. The crickets stopped their cricketing, and the whole Earth shook.

Then he came down again.

"Ha, ha," laughed Brown Pig. "That wasn't frightening at all. Stay with us. We are all as wild as you."

So the bear stayed.

A day later, it was the tiger's turn. His friends were stealing honey from the wild bees' nest when he stole up to them in the forest. The nest was deep in the darkest shade, and a steamy mist was creeping between the grey tree trunks. But even in the gloom, they could see Orange Tiger was crying.

"I know it is true," he said. "I cannot stay with you. I will make you very afraid. For the Fury of Tigers is coming over me, and I will roar and I will growl and run mad through the forest, breaking down the trees and killing the animals. I must go away."

"First go up to the mountain as we did, and let us see if you can make us afraid," said Red Dragon.

So Orange Tiger leaped up the hillside like a flame through the tall bamboo. And he danced like a dust devil on the mountain top.

He roared, he growled, he ran about snarling, and the whole Earth shook.

But when he came down again in the violet evening, his friends slapped him on the back and told him to stay.

"We are not afraid of you at all," said White Bear.

Chapter Three

Next morning, when Brown Pig told them he too was afraid he would scare them, the friends laughed so much they fell down.

"What will you do?" asked Old Man Shoa. "Will you run about grunting and squealing? Will you stamp on the grass and kill the ants? We are not afraid of you at all. Stay with us. We are going into the forest to look for wild garlic, and then we shall have a picnic."

So Brown Pig stayed.

On the fifth day, when the friends woke up, the sky was all dark. The birds had stopped singing. It was hot and sticky under the trees, and when the wind did blow it was rough and hard, and a sighing noise went all through the forest.

"It is all my fault," said Black Thunder. "I was afraid this might happen. All week long, while the rest of you have been boasting of how fierce and frightening you are, I have felt it inside me. It has been growing. Now it is going to burst out.

It is the Wrath of Storms. I must leave you at once, or I will shriek and howl and crash like a mad thing through the forest.

I will tear up the trees, I will blast the rocks, I will kill all the animals. I must go away."

His friends looked at him gravely. They knew that the Wrath of Storms could be a terrible thing.

"Well," said Old Man Shoa at last, looking down at his hands. "Why don't you do as the rest of them did? Go up to the top of the mountain and show us what you can do.

If we are truly afraid, then you can leave. If we are not, then stay with us and let's have no more of this nonsense."

With that, he walked off into the forest.

For, truth to tell, Old Man Shoa was becoming a little tired of his friends and their big talk about how very afraid everyone should be of them.

Right away, Black Thunder rose up into the sky like a dark bird. He stooped low over the mountain top. Suddenly, everything was still. A few fat drops of rain fell in the dust and spattered the leaves of the forest. Then with a great crash, the storm began.

Lightning tore the air, and the birds of the forest fled screeching from the trees. Thunder boomed and echoed in the hollows of the hillside. The rain was a grey curtain. The rivers rose and raged.

Old Man Shoa and the other four friends stood under a frangipani tree and shivered. But they weren't afraid. They were just cold. Actually, Old Man Shoa was annoyed.

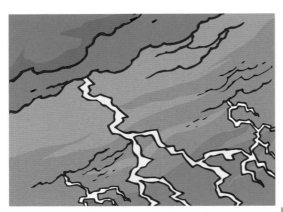

Chapter Four

When morning came, the air was clear again. The sun shone brighter than usual, and steam rose up from the forest trees and curled about the mountainside.

Old Man Shoa gathered the five friends together.

"I think we are agreed that Black Thunder should stay," he told them. "It was a good storm, but we were not really afraid."

The others nodded.

Then Old Man Shoa laughed, and it was not a very kind laugh.

"You do not know what fear is, you wild things with your growling and your roaring, your lightning and your thunder," he said. "And I am fed up with your noise. Come with me," he said, "And I will show you something you will never forget."

He took them through the forest to a flat place near a river, where no trees grew and the grass was long and golden from the sun.

"Bring tree trunks," Shoa told the friends. "Bring branches, and mud and grass."

Puzzled, the five friends did as they were asked. After they had made a big pile of tree trunks and branches and mud and grass, Old Shoa showed them some magic.

He built a house.

First, he dug four holes and stood four tree trunks in them, one at each corner. Then he used long grasses to tie poles and branches between the trunks and across the top of them for a roof. Next, he hung grass on the walls, and wove grass to make a roof. Lastly, he filled the cracks with mud and made a strong door of wood.

The five friends were astonished. They had never seen a house before.

"Go inside," said Old Man Shoa.

The five wild things went into the house. Shoa shut the door behind them.

It was very warm and very quiet inside the house. It was dark too, except where little chinks in the mud and grass let the sunlight through.

"Are you all right in there?" called Shoa. "You can come out in a second and see my surprise."

The friends said nothing. They did not like the house. Then they heard a strange sound.

CHINK, CLINK, KA-CHINK.

"What's that?" asked White Bear.

"Does it make you afraid?" came Old Man Shoa's voice from outside the house.

"Afraid?" said Red Dragon. "Afraid of a noise like that?"

CHINK, CLINK, KA-CHINK.

"We're not frightened of *that*!" laughed Brown Pig. "Let us out and let's go back to the forest."

"Yes," said Orange Tiger. "That is a little tiny noise. Why should it make us afraid?"

"Because," said Old Man Shoa, as he struck the flint against the steel again. "Because it is the sound of a person making fire."

CHINK, CLINK, KA-CHINK went the flint.

Now they heard a new sound, and all of a sudden they were really, truly afraid.

It was the sound of flames licking over dry grass, the sound of twigs crackling in a fire, the sound of leaves burning up in the hot air.

"What are you doing, Old Shoa?" called Orange Tiger. "Let us out, please."

Then Old Shoa laughed, and the friends feared he had gone mad. Frantically, they pushed against the door of the house to open it, but it was wedged shut with a branch and would not move.

Chapter Five

They could smell smoke now, and the sound of the flames was loud all around the house.

"It's burning," said White Bear. "The house is burning."

The crackle of fire was becoming a roar.

Outside, Old Man Shoa was stamping at the flames. Truly he hadn't expected his fire to spread through the grass like this. He had wanted to teach his friends a lesson, not burn down his new house with them inside it. But the fire was spreading too quickly.

Tongues of it were running up the side of the house, and a fountain of sparks went up from the roof.

With a great snarl of anger, Orange Tiger threw himself against the wall of the house.

The burning sticks made great black stripes on his side.

With a bellow of rage, White Bear jumped for the roof, and a cloud of scorching ash fell on him and turned him dark brown.

With a squeal of fury, Brown Pig rushed at the door, crashed into it, broke the hinges, and hurtled out into the sunlight.

As he passed the doorway, the flames burned his belly and the hairs on his skin turned yellow forever.

Then the thunder crashed and the dragon roared, and the house fell apart where it stood, and all the wild things ran into the forest in terror.

None of them ever came back. The tiger kept his stripes and lived in the stripy shade of the bird-loud forest. The brown bear stayed a brown bear, and he lived in a cave beside a waterfall. The wild pig has had yellow hair on his belly ever since. You can sometimes see him crashing around in the bamboo.

The dragon went up into the high sky and was never seen again. And the thunder went to live on the mountain top for good.

The fire burned for a day and a night. When it was out, Old Man Shoa rebuilt his house.

And although he sits up every night beside a smaller, tamer fire, looking out at the darkness or observing his shadow on the wall, none of the wild things has ever returned to visit him.

They are too afraid.